Biography of Olivia

Newton-John

The life story, career, family history,
achievements and death of the
Grammy-winning singer, Star of
Grease and Australia's heartbeat.

By

Danielle Dawson

Table of contents

INTRODUCTION

Olivia Newton-John dominated the silver screen, and therefore the signboard charts, and accomplished glorious humanitarian work throughout her career.

The celebrity worked diligently in Hollywood for several years, making a substantial internet price till her death in August 2022.

But it was her look as high school lady Sandy in the film Grease that launched her to international recognition.

The musical was the best box-office blockbuster of 1978 and provided Newton-John with 3 huge hit songs, together with you are the One That I would

like and Summer Nights, each performed
with co-star John Travolta.

And it was a spark for amendment in each of
her looks and her musical approach -
discarding her innocent, country-pop
persona.

Following the news of her passing, dozens of
admirers, further as notable personalities
from the planet of amusement, came to
depart meaningful comments and
recollections.

Actress Stockard Channing depicted Rizzo
in Grease - said: "I do not know whether or
not I've encountered a lovelier creature.

"Olivia was the embodiment of summer -
her lightness, her heat, and her class area
unit what perpetually involves my mind
after I think about her. I shall miss her
greatly."

Singer Rod Stewart delineates her as "the ideal girl, stunning, with wonderful class and with a precise Australian refinement".

"Her cloth pants in Grease were my inspiration for my 'Da you think that I am Sexy' part," he said, pertaining to the classic tight black apparel that she wore at the film's finale.

The US lead Oprah Winfrey expressed her "positivity was very contagious". "You'll be incomprehensible, Olivia," she wrote. "Here's to the happy days."

Travolta commented on Instagram: "Your influence was fantastic. I like you most. we have a tendency to shall meet you down the road and that we can all be along once more."

"Yours from the primary minute I met you and forever!" he continued, sign language off: "Your Danny, your John!"

The film's director Randal Kleiser claimed he had been familiar with Newton-John for forty years and "she ne'er modified, she was forever exactly the method everybody imagines her".

"She was tremendous, gorgeous, warm... such a big amount of clichés you would possibly say regarding their area unit, however in her instance, it absolutely was all real."

Asked what his enduring memory of her would be, he told: "Hanging out together with her at her ranch. Seeing the $64000 Olivia that was similar to the Olivia she was given. No cameras around, no individuals close... she was simply constant and as sweet as ever."

Other condolences came from singers Boomerang Minogue, who knew her as a concept, and Dionne Warwick, named Newton-John "one of the kindest people I had the pleasure of recording and singing with".

Chapter 1

Olivia Newton-John, the Australian singer whose breathy voice and natural beauty created her one of the best pop stars of the '70s and bewitched generations of viewers with the hit motion picture "Grease," died on Monday, in line with an announcement from her husband. She was 73.

"Dame Olivia Newton-John died quietly at her Ranch in Southern California this morning, encircled by family and friends.

We tend to raise that everybody please respect the family's privacy at this extraordinarily unhappy time," her husband, John Easterling, announced in a message on the singer's verified Instagram account.

"Olivia has been an emblem of achievements and hope for over thirty years chronicling her struggle with carcinoma."

The singer confirmed in Sept 2018 that she was fighting cancer at the bottom of her spine. It was her third cancer designation, once battling carcinoma between the early '90s and 2017.

Thanks to a run of country and soft-rock singles, Newton-John was already a distinguished vocalizer by the late Nineteen Seventies.

However, her co-starring performance aboard John Travolta in 1978's "Grease," presumably the foremost self-made motion picture musical of all time, propelled her to a replacement level of celebrity.

Though she had marginal acting expertise (and turned twenty-nine throughout the production), Newton-John made a picture performance as Sandy, a sweet-natured Australian transfer student who loves Travolta's alpha taco Danny at a Southern California high school within the Nineteen Fifties.

Their onscreen chemistry as mismatched lovebirds bear final-act makeovers to win each other's hearts — she swaps her ornate dresses for heels, leather, spandex, and a butt — anchored the motion picture and spurred repeat viewings by scores of admirers.

"I do not believe anybody may have anticipated a motion picture would persevere for forty years and would still achieve success and folks would still be returning to Maine regarding it all the time and adoring it," Newton-John stated in 2017.

"It's merely one in each of those movies. I am improbably blessed to possess a locality of it. It's brought such a big amount of individuals happiness."

Newton-John performed on 3 of the movie's greatest hits: the duets "You're The One That I Want" and "Summer Nights" with Travolta, and her swoony solo ballad, "Hopelessly dedicated to You."

Born in Cambridge, England in 1948, Newton-John resettled together with her family to Melbourne, Australia, once she was 5. Once winning a talent contest on a television show, "Sing, Sing, Sing," as an adolescent she created an all-girl ensemble and commenced functioning on weekly popular music shows in Australia.

Newton-John released her debut song in England in 1966 and had a couple of foreign successes, however, she remained principally unknown to North American country audiences till 1973, once "Let Maine Be There" became a top-10 smash on both the adult current and therefore the country charts.

A string of No. one easy-listening success followed, together with "I Honestly Love You," "Have You Ne'er Been Mellow" and "Please man. Please."

Then followed "Grease," which was 1978's top-grossing motion picture and has become an enduring cultural development.

The motion picture provided Newton-John an opportunity to remodel her squeaky-clean name. The duvet of her following album, "Totally Hot," depicted the vocalizer in black animal skin, whereas its tracks had an edgier, additional fashionable pop vibration.

In 1981, she took her new, sexier character a step further with "Physical," a dance routine with such provocative lyrics as, "There's nothing left to speak about until it's horizontally." Banned by some radio stations, it became her greatest success, spending 10 weeks atop the Billboard Hot 100.

She also acted in numerous more big-budget pictures, including the musical fantasy "Xanadu" starring Hollywood veteran Gene Kelly in his last film performance. The film underperformed, but its music sold well and yielded "Magic," a No. 1 hit.

In 1983 she joined with Travolta again for "Two of a Kind," a romantic comedy fantasy, but it failed to replicate their "Grease" spark.

Over a long career, Newton-John won four Grammy Awards and sold more than 100 million CDs.

"I've lived numerous lives in music. I had country initially when I began, then I moved over into pop," she said. "I had 'Xanadu' and 'Grease,' many tunes in between. I feel really thankful. I have such a broad repertoire to pick from."

Chapter 2

Olivia has been a symbol of achievements and hope for over 30 years chronicling her struggle with breast cancer.

Her therapeutic inspiration and pioneering experience with plant medicine continue with the Olivia Newton-John Foundation Fund, committed to investigating plant medicine and cancer.

Newton-John's daughter, Chloe Lattanzi, paid homage to her mother with a collection of photographs on Instagram, including pictures of Lattanzi as a newborn.

After her initial cancer diagnosis, Newton-John became a renowned crusader, setting up the Olivia Newton-John Cancer and Wellness Research Centre in Melbourne.

Her popularity as an activist for research and improved treatment will certainly remain as vital a feature of her legacy as her Hollywood career, which includes four Grammy victories and the selling of more than 100m albums.

Born in Cambridge, England, in 1948, Newton-John and her family immigrated to Melbourne, Australia, when she was six.

Yet she remained proud of her roots: her father was an MI5 officer who worked on the Enigma project at Bletchley Park during the war; her maternal grandfather was the Nobel prize-winning scientist Max Born, who sought refuge in the UK from Nazi Germany on the eve of the second world war.

At 14, Newton-John started her professional singing career, recording her first single in 1966 on a return trip to England, and her first solo album, If Not For You, in 1971.

A short career drop followed the album's early popularity, but Newton-John represented the UK in the 1974 Eurovision song contest; her song, Long Live Love, ended joint fourth behind Abba's winning Waterloo. Then came a time of performing and recording country music, before she was cast in Grease.

The shift her character endures in the film – from a strait-laced darling to a spandex-clad goer – inspired a similar swerve in Newton-John's musical career, culminating in her 1981 album Physical.

A second collaboration with Travolta, on the 1983 film Two of a Kind, failed, but the duo remained close friends during the following decades, and most recently performed together in 2012.

A series of musical comebacks met with varying degrees of success during the previous four decades, which were also spent fighting sickness, raising a daughter, Chloe, and working in the realms of health, the environment, and animal rights.

"Cancer was enlightening," she said in 2012. "When you're unwell, it doesn't matter if you have all the money in the world — it makes no difference. I feel incredibly grateful to have been allowed to live."

Newton-John is survived by her husband, John Easterling, founder of natural remedies brand Amazon Herb Company, and her daughter, Chloe Rose Lattanzi.

Chapter 3

In a statement, the hospital that manages the Olivia Newton-John Cancer Wellness and Research Centre in Melbourne - which was created following the star's activism - said she "encouraged, inspired and supported" staff and patients daily.

"We are immensely appreciative of the great friendship we enjoyed with Olivia for many years. Her kind support and donation offered hope and improved the lives of hundreds of cancer sufferers... She was the light at the end of the tunnel for many, many others."

Her accomplishments in the area were honored by Queen Elizabeth, who recognized her with a damehood in the 2020 New Year's Honours list.

In a statement uploaded on her social media platforms, Newton-husband John's John Easterling announced she had died on Monday as he celebrated her as "a symbol of victory and hope for over 30 years sharing her experience with breast cancer".

"Her therapeutic inspiration and pioneering experience with plant medicine continues through the Olivia Newton-John Foundation Fund, committed to investigating plant medicine and cancer."

Her breast cancer diagnosis prompted her to postpone and cancel multiple trips.

And in 2005 Newton-then-boyfriend, John's Patrick McDermott, vanished at sea while on a fishing expedition off the coast of California. He was never discovered — a mystery that tormented the singer for years.

It's really hard to live with that," she told in 2006. "It's the toughest thing I've ever experienced, and I've gone through a lot of things."

Although her commercial reputation waned in her latter years, Newton-John never ceased recording and performing. Among her achievements were guest performances on "Glee," a long-running "Summer Nights" engagement at the Flamingo Las Vegas, and a dance-club smash, "You Have to Believe," recorded with daughter Chloe.

"I love to sing, it's all I know how to do," she told in 2017. "That's all I've ever done since I was 15, so it's my life. I am pleased that I can still do it and people still come to see me."

It was absorbing my day and after a while, I decided 'you know what, I need to live my life so I'm going to eat a cookie if I want it," she added.

"Because the pleasure of life and daily living needs to be a part of that healing process as well. That I've chosen that way to be appreciative and to feel good about things because the other side's not so wonderful.

In 2017, Newton-John disclosed the breast cancer she had previously experienced in 1992 had returned and had spread to her spine. She also disclosed she'd gotten a second cancer diagnosis in 2013 but had kept it private. She claimed she thought she would "win over it" and urged her home Australia to follow the rules of the US state where she then resided, California, to legalize the therapeutic use of marijuana.

"My desire is that in Australia soon, it will be accessible to all the cancer patients and individuals suffering through a disease that causes pain," she added, adding that despite she had periods of despair, she had had "a fantastic career" and "nothing to complain about".

Newton-John remained a regular hitmaker during the following several years, notably on the Adult Contemporary and Country charts.

Behind the scenes, however, Newton-John found herself entangled in a struggle with her record company, MCA, that had huge ramifications for the music business.

Invoking a section of California labor law known as the "seven-year rule," Newton-John launched a $10 million lawsuit against MCA and was finally allowed to depart the company.

In response, the record business urged the California state government to adopt regulations to allow them to sue musicians for "lost profits" if they didn't meet album obligations or other contractual components, making it tougher for future artists to leave arrangements as Newton-John had.

While Newton-John was fighting MCA, she was simultaneously experiencing one of the most significant stages of her career and pop culture history in general.

The cinematic version of the great Broadway musical, Grease, had become a huge phenomenon. Meanwhile, its soundtrack became one of the best-selling albums of the year, anchored by Travolta and Newton-John's Number One blockbuster, "You're the One That I Want."

In a Rolling Stone feature from that year, Newton-John commented about how being cast as Sandy dramatically transformed the way she saw her career. "The film folks were constantly treating me as Sandy, this

17-year-old naïve woman, who wasn't actually me. Well, some of it was," she responded.

"One day — the day before we were meant to film the scene that features Sandy's transition — I showed up like the 'other' girl and they all hit on me! I asked myself, 'What have I been doing wrong?' This side is considerably more enjoyable than the lovely, virginal side! ... [It] was an opening up for me. I felt from it that I wanted to attempt various things. I was open to anything new."

Chapter 4

Newton-John embraced her new persona entirely as she entered the Eighties.

While her following picture, Xanadu, didn't approach the heights of Grease, the film's soundtrack nevertheless contained a couple of successes, including another Newton-John Number One, "Magic," and her duet with Electric Light Orchestra on the title track.

The next year, Newton-John earned her career-defining smash, an openly daring pop gem that seems inextricable from the Eighties workout craze.

With MTV on the rise, "Physical" also received a significant boost from its exciting music video, in which Newton-John helps a group of out-of-shape and overweight guys become amazingly ripped.

In 1983, Newton-John and Travolta returned for Two of a Kind, which, like Xanadu, bombed at the box office and with critics, but enjoyed a hugely popular soundtrack.

As the Eighties passed, Newton-John was unable to retain the same degree of popularity, while remaining a celebrity and pop cultural icon. She utilized her position to advocate for a variety of humanitarian concerns, such as the United Nations Environment Program.

After being diagnosed with, and fighting, breast cancer in the early Nineties, Newton-John became a prominent backer of efforts to aid individuals suffering from the illness (when her cancer returned later in life, she became an outspoken advocate for medical marijuana).

Newton-John also adapted her experience with cancer into an album, 1994's Gaia: One Woman's Journey.

Throughout the Nineties and into the 2000s, Newton-John continued to concentrate on charity causes, while still having plenty of time for music, film, and television.

She turned up as a guest star on several TV series, including two cameos on Glee, one of which had her recreating the "Physical" video with Jane Lynch.

She continued to travel frequently as well and performed numerous successful Las Vegas residencies throughout the 2010s. Just last year, Newton-John and her daughter, Chloe Lattanzi, recorded a song together, "Window in the Wall."

"Listen, I believe every day is a blessing," Newton-John told in 2020 as she pondered on her career and her repeated bouts with cancer. "You never know when your time is done; we all have a certain amount of time in this world, and we simply need to be thankful for that."

Newton-John married her Xanadu co-star Matt Lattanzi in 1984. They had a daughter, Chloe Rose, in 1986, and they subsequently announced their separation in April 1995.

The artist endured another setback in June 2005. Her lover of nine years, Patrick McDermott, 48, disappeared after he failed to return from a fishing trip off the California coast. There were several inquiries regarding McDermott's odd disappearance, with some alleging that he was still alive and residing in Mexico.

Three years later, Newton-John married American entrepreneur John Easterling. The bride and husband attended a secret Incan spiritual ceremony on a mountainside near Cuzco, Peru, on June 21, 2008, followed by a second, legal wedding on June 30 on Jupiter Island, Florida.

Easterling is the creator and president of Amazon Herb Company, which distributes botanical supplements from the jungle. The pair met via a friend more than 15 years previous to their wedding but didn't become romantically linked until 2007, according to People magazine. They stayed married until her death.

Chapter 5

Despite her academic background, early on Olivia showed an interest in singing, establishing a band called the Sol Four with her school friends, and later on performing at her brother-in-law's coffee cafe in Australia.

She participated in various Australian TV series such as The Go Show as a teenager she acted in the movie Funny Things Happen Down Under which was forgettable save from some early potential seen in Olivia's lovely performance of "Christmas Down Under".

A talent contest held by the Australian Johnny O'Keefe gave Olivia the reward of a vacation to England, and she took this up in 1965. Her first exposure to creating recordings was a one-off single agreement with Decca Records.

The single, Till You Say You'll Be Mine/For Ever, is incredibly uncommon however these two tracks were released (Oct 1994) on the British collection CD Pop Inside the '60s.

England did not make Olivia fully happy - she missed Australia and her then lover, Ian Turpie. In one interview she describes how she tried to arrange her return journey without alerting her mother, who had accompanied her to the UK.

Fortunately for Olivia's followers and her future profession her mother was not having her daughter miss this chance to widen her horizons and Olivia's ambitions were blocked.

Things improved when Pat Carroll, a fellow Australian, arrived in the UK. Dreaming of fame the two females toured pubs and clubs as the singing pair creatively dubbed "Pat and Olivia". New to the British music industry their early hirings were not always a success - such as the duo's appearance at Paul Raymond's Revue club.

They were rather caught away by the skimpy clothes of some of the other artists. Needless to say, the couple who were dressed in high-necked frilly gowns were not invited back to what they, later on, found was a strip bar.

In 1968 Bruce Welch of the Shadows fell for Olivia and they were engaged, something which was not totally without complications since he was married at the time.

Pat's visa ran out in December 1969 and she went home. For Olivia, cinematic glory awaited when she was approached to join the band Toomorrow, which was to be Britain's equivalent to the Monkees.

This artificial ensemble published an eponymous album in 1970 to coincide with the picture Toomorrow, but the audience was not enthused and the movie closed abruptly, allowing Olivia to focus on her solo music career.

Olivia was selected to be the resident star for Cliff Richard's hugely popular TV program in 1972, and she was a frequent live performer in London.

The early Seventies was a fruitful era for Olivia - her partnership with Cliff Richard and the Shadows propelled her music to a large audience. Cliff Richard had a regular TV program and Olivia was a frequent guest. She published the albums Olivia

Newton-John (1971), and Olivia (1972), Music Makes My Day (1973).

Bruce Welch orchestrated Olivia's first hit song, a rendition of Bob Dylan's If Not For You. This track was Olivia's first taste of success in America, something she was to enjoy a lot more of in the coming several years.

Olivia marked a turning point in her career with the release of Let Me Be There which peaked at #6 in America. No longer engaged to Bruce Welch, John Farrar, another member of the Shadows, took up composition and arrangement for her and this was a successful combo that was shortly to take the United States by storm.

John Farrar had known Olivia from the early days and he subsequently married Pat Carroll, Olivia's former singing companion, and eventual business partner.

While holidaying in 1974 in the South of France, Olivia met Lee Kramer, who had a thriving commercial import/export firm. The relationship evolved, and Lee remained Olivia's lover and manager for most of the remainder of the decade.

Just before she relocated to the United States to capitalize on her blossoming fame there, Olivia represented the UK in the Eurovision Song Contest in 1974. Both music and Olivia's attire on the night were picked by a vote of TV viewers, and the entire jumble illustrated precisely what was wrong with vox pop artistic taste.

A genuinely dreadful oompah - oompah song, Long Live Love was picked, combined with a long flowing baby-blue attire for the actual performance.

This time Olivia was up against heavy competition - 1974 was the year that ABBA stole the show with a barnstorming performance of their song "Waterloo", which began their worldwide fame. Olivia came fourth.

America called and Olivia departed England in 1975 to a euphoric reception for her second album "Have You Never Been Mellow". The title song hit #1 and her following single from the album, Please Mr. Please, reached #3.

This was the start of a roll that lasted throughout the 70s with a streak of gold albums in the US. Olivia was to become a regular on programs like the Midnight Special, and in 1976 she had her TV special by ABC - A Very Special Olivia Newton-John.

Her US audience had appreciated her for her soft and delicate delivery of ballads and country tunes, and she rewarded them with a succession of CDs exquisitely delivered - Clearly Love, Come On Over, Don't Stop Believin, and Making a Good Thing Better. Olivia visited the United States with the album Clearly Love.

Olivia captivated hearts in Japan with her vocals as well as in the US - she visited Japan in 1976 with the album Don't Stop Believin'. Japanese audiences have liked her since her appearance at the 1971 Tokyo Music Fair, and the 1976 concert was published as a live CD in Japan named 'Love Performance'.

She earned a run of Grammys for her work, and lived in Malibu, near Los Angeles, with a property in the foothills.

There she accomplished a childhood desire, maintaining a lot of dogs and horses on the farm. As a youngster, she had not been able to have many pets despite her love of animals. Her commitment to animal welfare spilled over into her work life when she refused to travel to Japan unless they altered tuna fishing tactics to prevent the senseless murder of dolphins in the nets.

After reaching the zenith of her career with Physical, Olivia decided to take things simpler. She was starting to think about other directions - one of them was starting a store with Australian novelties, which was later to turn into the "Koala Blue" fashion chain.

To recapture the box-office magic of 'Grease', Olivia was paired alongside John Travolta in the movie Two of a Kind.

In interviews at the time, Olivia said that this was her first opportunity to star in a non-musical movie, but the result was not a cinematic success. Once again, though, the soundtrack of Two of a Kind did pretty well with several excellent tunes by Olivia and a delightful duet with John Travolta.

Olivia married her young live-in partner Matt Lattanzi, around Christmas 1984, after they had lived together for four years. The couple had a beautiful honeymoon in Paris.

Her next shift in musical direction was the sultry risqué approach of "Soulkiss" ; it was not a musical triumph. Bizarrely, the videogram was taken while Olivia was pregnant with daughter Chloe - attempting not to indicate this hampered the creative flexibility of the filmmaker slightly.

The CD, which portrayed Olivia in tight riding trousers and boots clutching a crop on the back cover, pushed things farther than the audience believed plausible.

Chapter 6

Chloe was born in early 1986, and this caused a break in Olivia's music. The period 1986 to 1992 was lean in her entertainment career, as she dedicated herself to motherhood, and to developing her business venture, the Koala Blue chain of stores.

Olivia transformed her original idea for an Australian specialty store into a fashion chain. This venture was created with fellow Australian and the wife of Olivia's long-time record producer, Pat Farrar, with whom Olivia had started out singing in Britain in the late Sixties and early Seventies.

Koala Blue intended to be a more family-friendly alternative to a rigorous singing career, but it did not endure the late '80s/early '90s recession. Olivia elected to grow the franchise network precisely as customers were cutting their spending on non-essentials, and the firm filed for bankruptcy amid some recriminations.

Music was not wholly disregarded – in 1988, Olivia brought out "The Rumour", with the title single composed by Elton John. 1988 was also the year of the Australian Bicentennial, and Olivia did a videogram named "Down Under" for the Rumour, in which she played the songs in some gorgeous Australian surroundings.

The Australian edition of the album has the song "It's Always Australia For Me" which is omitted from foreign versions.

Warm And Tender, launched in 1989, was not actually designed for the mainstream pop industry. An album of children's songs and lullabies, this was intended for Chloe. It is Olivia's first real musical indulgence, which was released on the Geffen label after MCA refused to run it.

Geffen released "Back To Basics, The Essential Collection" in 1992. This was to be Olivia's return to what she did best, a retrospective of her career but included four new songs, which Olivia marketed extensively, and she was practicing to go on tour with the album in the late summer.

The news came on July 2 - Olivia Newton-John had breast cancer. She was rushed to the hospital and operated on, and then had to endure a term of chemotherapy. In February the following year, she received the all-clear and traveled to Australia to heal.

Gaia, One Woman's Journey, an incredibly intimate and cheerful CD, was one of the fruits of Olivia's time in Australia away from the spotlight.

The record was not released in the United States but was widely circulated on indie labels worldwide. Olivia opted to share her experiences with breast cancer so that other women in a similar circumstance might understand that survival was possible and that early identification was vital.

After her recuperation, there were rumors of problems in Olivia's marriage, which came to a climax in 1995 with the revelation that Olivia and her husband Matt Lattanzi, were to go their separate ways and ultimately divorce.

For the next two years, Olivia's career was a medley of different directions, with her participating in beauty ads for Home Shopping, a bit part in a US sitcom, an Australian wildlife show titled "Human Nature", appearing in an Aussie TV series "The Man From Snowy River" and acting in the movie "It's My Party" directed by Grease director Randal Kleiser.

After two years of wandering in the wilderness professionally, Olivia began to feel her way musically once again, with some fine singing for the US Christmas movie "Snowden on Ice", and some private performances at events for CHEC, a charity dear to Olivia's heart.

In July 1997 MCA-Nashville contracted Olivia for a pop country album, and she recorded a duet with the Raybon Bros "Falling" for their namesake album.

"Back With a Heart" released in May 1998, finds Olivia in terrific form with a wonderful combination of pop and country.

Teaming up with Cliff Richard in her first live performance for many years, Australian audiences were treated to Cliff and Olivia live in February and March 1998. The end of 1998 saw Olivia join two Australians for the Main Event Tour, a sellout event with more dates added by popular demand.

It was America's time in 1999 - beginning on New Year's Eve 98/99 with a mini-tour Olivia entertained fans with a set of her biggest songs, followed by a much bigger tour of the United States in the summer.

Meanwhile, a fresh appearance and a new direction beckoned, with an acting part in Del Shores' independent production of the stage drama Sordid Lives.

A new century brought a 14-date American tour in the spring/early Summer with a fresh line-up of songs from her Greatest Hits. Fans in Asia were also excited to see Olivia playing in Hong Kong and Korea throughout the Summer.

The Fall of 2000 saw Olivia singing to her largest audience yet - performing a duet with Australian superstar John Farnham at the Opening Ceremonies of the Sydney Olympic Games. She also performed live at Australia's Carols By Candlelight on Christmas Eve.

In April 2008 Olivia walked the Great Wall of China, all of 228km, to raise donations for her Olivia Newton-John Cancer Centre's Wellness Centre.

She was accompanied by a variety of friends and celebrities including Sir Cliff Richard, Joan Rivers, Leeza Gibbons, Didi Conn, Dannii Minogue, and Amy Sky. She published the uplifting A Celebration of Song CD with earnings going towards her Cancer & Wellness Centre.

The same year Olivia's 2006 performance at Sydney Opera House was published on DVD and shown on the PBS network to great acclaim. Olivia co-hosted various episodes of Healing Quest for PBS in line with her beliefs in the natural healing potential of the body.

Her next appearance in A Few Best Men made something of a sensation, not only as it had Olivia's character behaving outrageously but also was to generate a CD soundtrack that displayed a musical side to Olivia that fans had not seen before.

Dance remixes of vintage pop tracks reworked by DJs like Chew Fu, Roulette, and Archiesuch. The lyrics to the Toni Basil hit Mikey Olivia noted were much risqué than anyone seemed to have noticed before! Olivia also recorded a new song Weightless penned by her long-time producer John Farrar and his son Max.

An Australian TV movie about her life has been in the process for a few years. Olivia granted hesitant assent for this to be manufactured, they were going to make it anyhow so Olivia said she'd co-operate provided her revenues went to her Cancer and Wellness Centre.

The movie helped that it featured her dear friend Delta Goodrem and she recorded two of her songs as duets with Delta, one of which is the wonderful Love Is A Gift. The TV movie was eventually released on DVD but Olivia has yet to view it, no doubt her inherent shyness and seclusion make this impossible.

However, the TV movie was an incentive to write her long-anticipated autobiography called Don't Stop Believin', titled after one of Olivia's successes. This was warmly lauded by fans and the media alike and became a New York Best Seller.

The previous few years have conferred on Olivia various honors, in 2018 she obtained the Honorary Doctorate of Letters from La Trobe University in Melbourne.

In 2019 she earned the Companion (AC) of the Order of Australia (General Division), which is the highest Australian award.

At the end of 2019, she was made a Dame Commander of the Order of the British Empire by Her Majesty the Queen, becoming Dame Olivia Newton-John. These honors are in honor of her dedication to music, cancer research, and philanthropy.

In 2019 Olivia planned an auction of some of her apparel and memorabilia to be auctioned off to benefit her Cancer and Wellness Centre.

Her famed leather jacket from the last scene of Grease was auctioned for a stunning

$405,000, in a lovely unexpected twist the unknown buyer of the garment returned it to Olivia. Therefore, Olivia got to retain the jacket (it may in the future be exhibited at her Cancer and Wellness Centre) and her Centre still profited from the earnings!

2020 into 2021 may be an era when the globe is closed down but Olivia continues to compose music and talk about the advantages of plant remedies.

Olivia's January 2021 release of Window In The Wall single with daughter Chloe continues the women's efforts to promote compassion and love.

2021 started a cooperation with Primary Wave Work Publishing to offer her music to a broader audience.

The well-renowned producer, remixer, and composer Vinny Vero are now working on remastering and digitalizing her work for future releases. The original edition of this was for the Physical album's 40th anniversary - an expanded Deluxe album combined with a DVD was re-released in October 2021.

Chapter 7

Olivia has always had a sense of Nature and the living environment. She always had a penchant for maintaining animals and is a talented horse rider. At her Malibu house, she had quite a zoo of dogs and horses, and other pets.

This affection for nature is also evident in her music - as early as her 1976 Come On Over album there was a song on 'wild horses galloping free' and her 1981 Physical album had the extraordinarily delicate 'Dolphin Song'.

She became United Nations ambassador for the Environment on the UNEP program and sang in the 'Spirit of the Forest' cooperation in the early eighties. Her 1994 album, Gaia, has a significant environmental message.

With the birth of Chloe, it was not unexpected that such a sensitive person as Olivia would also devote herself to initiatives affecting children.

Olivia has co-written a children's book called 'A Pig Tale' with an environmental message. She was also actively engaged in the Colette Chuda Environmental Fund (now Healthy Child Healthy World).

According to Celebrity Net Worth, the estimated net worth Newton-John left behind was $60 million.

In lieu of flowers, the family requests that any contributions be given in her memory to the Olivia Newton-John Foundation Fund.'
The charity sponsors research into plant-based medicine and holistic cancer therapies.

Chloe shared a touching homage to her mother on Instagram three days ago, saying: 'I adore this lady. My mum. My best friend.'

Olivia is survived by her husband John Easterling; daughter Chloe Lattanzi; sister Sarah Newton-John; brother Toby Newton-John; nieces and nephews Tottie, Fiona, and Brett Goldsmith; Emerson, Charlie, Zac, Jeremy, Randall, and Pierz Newton-John; Jude Newton-Stock, Layla Lee; Kira and Tasha Edelstein; and Brin and Valerie Hall."

With a career spanning more than five decades, 100 million albums sold, four Grammy Awards, ten #1 successes, and over 15 top 10 songs, Newton-John has well and thoroughly earned her spot as one of the world's most successful performers.

She was also granted an Order Of The British Empire by Queen Elizabeth in 1979, an Order of Australia in 2006, and again in 2019.

In 2018 she also earned an Honorary Doctorate of Letters from La Trobe University in Melbourne, in appreciation of her major and continuous support of cancer research and holistic health.

It was in December 2019 that Her Majesty the Queen made Newton-John a Dame Commander of the Order of the British Empire for her contributions to music, cancer research, and charity.

Up to her departure, Newton-John was living on a property just outside of Santa Barbara with her husband, Easterling.

Newton-John famously said: "I just have a beautiful life, a really blessed existence."

While Chloe has been pretty upfront about the fact that she underwent botched cosmetic surgery at the age of 18, the 36-year-old was also hooked on cocaine and Xanax.

Now, she is primarily against Western medication, and her mother revealed that she was pain-free due to legal cannabis.

Lattanzi has also talked about eating disorders since she experienced the anguish of having one.

She states that her fiancé and her mother aided her through rehabilitation.

While her parents split in 1995, Lattanzi has been fortunate in love.
She maintains a legal cannabis farm in Oregon with her fiancé James Driskill, to whom she's been engaged since 2010.

During her interview, Olivia stated she would "try not" to worry about dying.
She confessed: "I mean, it's part of life. And, of course, if you get a cancer diagnosis, your death is sort of there.

"Whereas most people, we don't have an idea when we're gonna die. And I could die tomorrow — a tree may fall on me. So, it's only that we have the knowledge that we may die.

"But I try not to worry about it too much, but I try to meditate and be calm about it, and know that everyone I love is there, so there's something to look forward to."

Just days before her death at age 73, Olivia Newton-John shared a tragic farewell post with her husband, John Easterling.

The shot was uploaded on August 5, only three days before Newton-terrible John's demise.

Captioned "#FlashbackFriday" with a love emoji, the snapshot depicts the Grease actress with her husband, John Easterling.

Facts you didn't know about Olivia

1. Olivia Newton-John Said Her Daughter Gives Her Strength & They Recorded a Song Together, 'Window on the Wall'

Newton-John told the TODAY program that her daughter, Chloe Rose Lattanzi, gives her strength. In the 2021 interview, the star spoke about quarantine and the birth of the mother-daughter partnership.

"The song just called me, I wasn't looking for it. And then I played the music and I began bawling. It was incredibly emotional, the song truly touched me in the gut," she stated on the broadcast.

Newton-John claimed she composed the song and thought her daughter was the perfect person to pair with for the duet.

"It was about relationships, it was about forgiveness, compassion, seeing the other side, other people's point of view, and yet with love. And understanding and kindness," she stated.

Lattanzi remarked on the program that she was touched by her mother's plea.

"And I loved how affected my mom was, and the fact that she could've picked anybody to sing it with her and she asked me, it touched my heart more than you could ever know," she told.

2. Newton-John Was the Granddaughter of a Nobel Prize Winner Who Was Friends With Albert Einstein

Newton-John's mother, Irene, was the daughter of Max Born. Born was a physicist who was given the Nobel prize.

The German scientist was given the Nobel Prize for Physics in 1954, resulting from his laboratory research at the University of Frankfurt-on-Main when he was named professor in 1919, at the onset of World War I, according to The Nobel Prize website.

Much of his work centered on crystals and crystal lattices. Born was the son of an embryologist and anatomist, who was married in 1913 and had three children.

"As were such a large number of alternative German scientists, he was duty-bound to flee in 1933 and was welcome to Cambridge, wherever he lectured for 3 years as Stokes Lecturer," the storynadded. "His major sector of study throughout this era was within the field of nonlinear electrodynamics, which he created in partnership with Infeld."

3. Newton-John's Father Was an M15 Agent UN agency who arrested Nazi Leader Rudolph Hess

Olivia Newton-John was born in Cambridge, England, on Sept twenty-six, 1948, to folks Brinley "Bryn" Newton-John and Irene Born.

The family moved to Melbourne, Australia, once she was six. There, her father worked as an academic. Before that, her father was additionally an AN M15 agent.

Brinley Newton-John was AN MI5 agent at the UN agency who worked on the Enigma project at Bletchley Park, in keeping with his announcement.

He was additionally called the agent who took Nazi leader Rudolph Hess into custody throughout world war II. His partner and Newton-John's mother, Irene Newton-John, was a Jewish war expatriate.

He, too, died of cancer, according to the obituary. His reason for death was cancer of the liver in 1992. Brinley Newton-John was seventy-eight at the time of his death.

4. Newton-John Was the Youngest of three youngsters & Her Sister Married 'Grease' Co-Star Jeff Conaway

Newton-John has 2 elder siblings, a report said. Her brother, Hugh, was a doctor whereas her sister, Rona, followed AN acting career. Rona Newton-John was married to her sister's co-star in Grease, Jeff Conaway, for 5 years, from 1980 to 1985.

Rona Newton-John additionally died from cancer, according to a source. She was seventy years old once she died from brain cancer in March 2013, the story claimed.

Rona Newton-John remarried, marrying Melbourne entrepreneur and spot mogul Brian Goldsmith, the newspaper expressed. She had four children: skilled racing car driver author Newton-John, singer Tottie Goldsmith, Brett Goldsmith, and Fiona Edelstein.

"While she spent a lot of her childhood within the shadow of her younger sister's quality, Rona had many acting opportunities together with appearances on The comedian Show and also the British tv series Gerry Anderson's phantasm," the report claimed. The sisters additionally recorded a duet, "Just U.S.A. 2."

5. Two of Newton-John's relations Grow Marijuana & She Was an Advocate for Medical Cannabis

Newton-John became AN advocate for medicative cannabis once she was exposed to that by her husband, John Easterling.

"I was frightened about it from the start. However, I saw the enhancements when I started taking it. It helps with worry, it helps with sleep, it helps with pain," Newton-John told the outlet.

Easterling produces marijuana on their ranch, and his output within the greenhouse is a component of his company, the Amazon Herb Company. Lattanzi incorporates a marijuana plantation in Oregon, the story added.

Printed in Great Britain
by Amazon

86591954R00041